Impressum

Verlag: BABADADA GmbH, Nedderfeld 112 , 22529 Hamburg

Geschäftsführer / Verlagsleitung: Harald Hof

Druck: Books on Demand GmbH, In de Tarpen 42, 22848 Norderstedt

Imprint

Publisher: BABADADA GmbH, Nedderfeld 112 , 22529 Hamburg, Germany

Managing Director / Publishing direction: Harald Hof

Print: Books on Demand GmbH, In de Tarpen 42, 22848 Norderstedt

学校
school

割り算
divide

186/2

黒板
board

教室
classroom

校庭
school yard

教師
teacher

紙
paper

書く
write

ペン
pen

事務机
desk

定規
ruler

本
book

生徒
pupil

ランドセル

satchel

筆入れ

pencil case

鉛筆

pencil

鉛筆削り

pencil sharpener

消しゴム

rubber

スケッチブック

drawing pad

スケッチ
drawing

絵筆
paintbrush

絵の具箱
paint box

はさみ
scissors

接着剤
glue

練習帳
exercise book

宿題
homework

12

数
number

2+2

足し算
add

5-2

引き算
subtract

2×2

かけ算
multiply

計算する
calculate

A

文字
letter

ABCDEFG
HIJKLMN
OPQRSTU
VWXYZ

アルファベット
alphabet

単語
word

テキスト

text

読む

read

チョーク

chalk

授業

lesson

学級日誌

register

試験

examination

通知表

certificate

制服

school uniform

教育

education

百科事典

encyclopedia

大学

university

顕微鏡

microscope

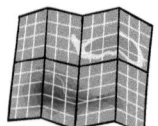

地図

map

ごみ箱

waste-paper basket

旅行

travel

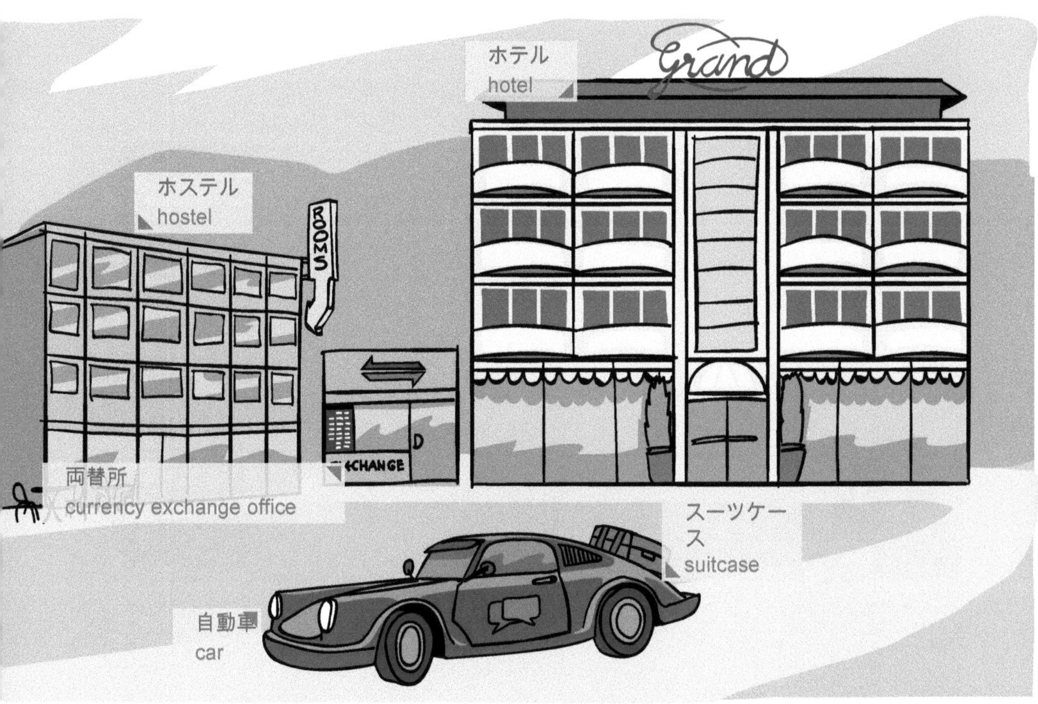

ホテル
hotel
Grand
ホステル
hostel
ROOMS
両替所
currency exchange office
スーツケース
suitcase
自動車
car

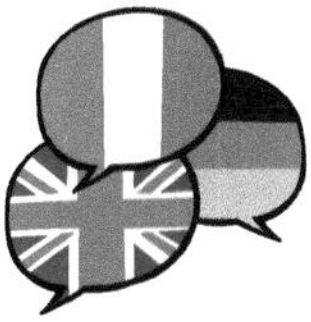

言語

language

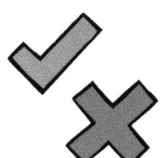

はい / いいえ

yes / no

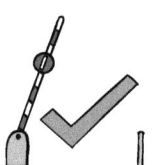

問題ない

Okay

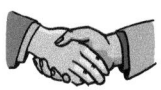

ハロー

hello

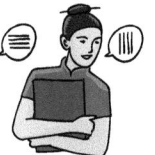

翻訳者

translator

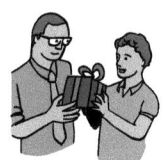

ありがとう

Thank you

...はいくらですか？

how much is...?

わかりません

I don't get it

問題

problem

こんばんは！

Good evening!

おはようございます！

Good morning!

おやすみなさい！

Good night!

さようなら

goodbye

方向

direction

手荷物

luggage

バッグ

bag

リュックサック

backpack

お客様

guest

部屋

room

寝袋

sleeping bag

テント

tent

旅行者情報

tourist information

ビーチ

beach

クレジットカード

credit card

朝食

breakfast

昼食

lunch

夕食

dinner

チケット

Ticket

エレベーター

elevator

スタンプ

stamp

境界

border

税関

customs

大使館

embassy

ビザ

visa

パスポート

passport

輸送

transport

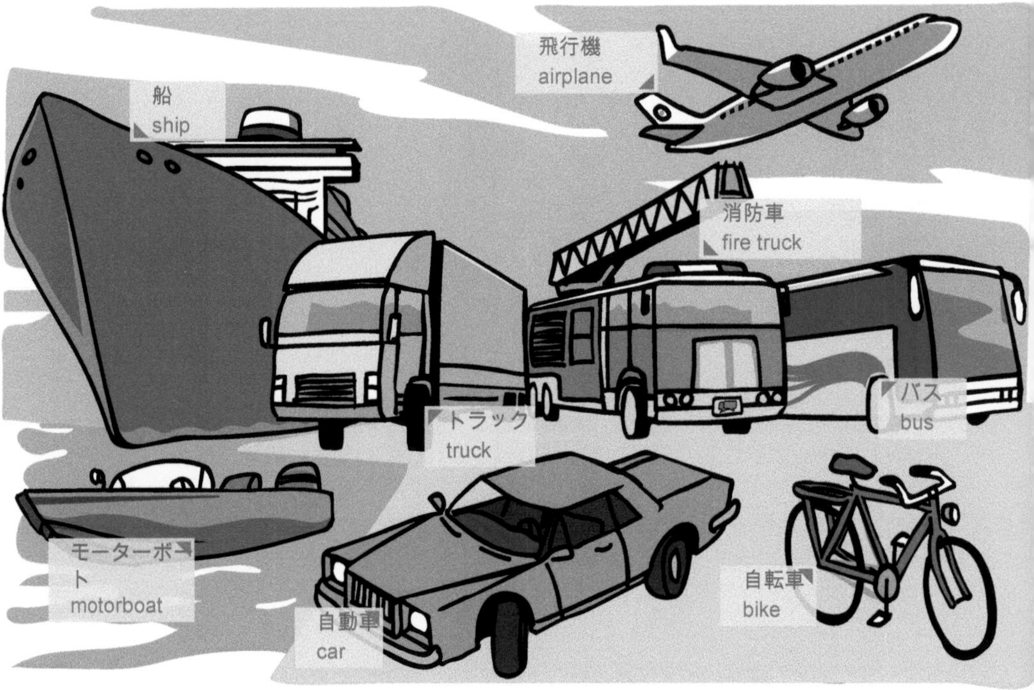

飛行機
airplane
船
ship
消防車
fire truck
バス
bus
トラック
truck
モーターボート
motorboat
自動車
car
自転車
bike

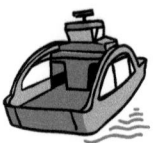

フェリー

ferry

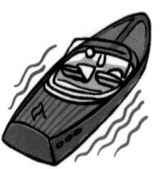

ボート

boat

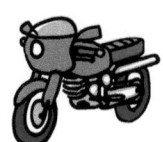

バイク

motorbike

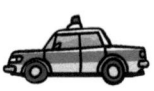

パトカー

police car

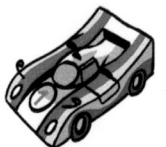

レーシングカー

racing car

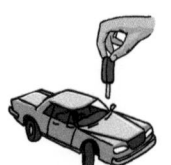

レンタカー

rental car

カーシェアリング

car sharing

レッカー車

tow truck

ごみ収集車

garbage truck

モーター

engine

燃料

fuel

ガソリンスタンド

fuel station

交通標識

traffic sign

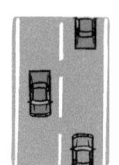

交通

traffic

渋滞

traffic jam

駐車場

parking lot

駅

train station

道

tracks

列車

train

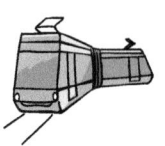

路面電車

tram

車両

wagon

ヘリコプター

helicopter

空港

airport

タワー

tower

乗客

passenger

コンテナ

container

段ボール箱

carton

カート

cart

カゴ

basket

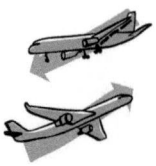

離陸 / 着陸

take off / land

都市

city

村

village

都心

city center

家

house

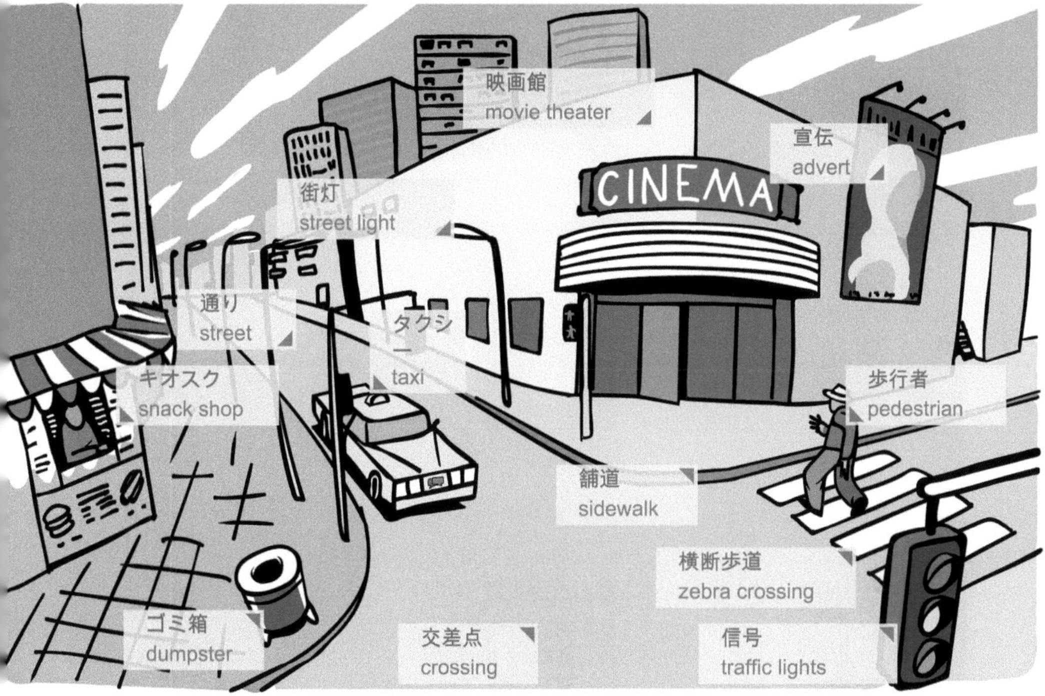

映画館
movie theater
宣伝
advert
CINEMA
街灯
street light
通り
street
タクシー
taxi
キオスク
snack shop
歩行者
pedestrian
舗道
sidewalk
横断歩道
zebra crossing
ゴミ箱
dumpster
交差点
crossing
信号
traffic lights

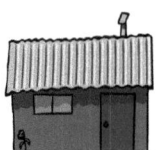

小屋

hut

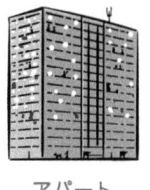

アパート

apartment

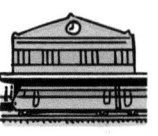

駅

train station

市役所

city hall

MUSEUM

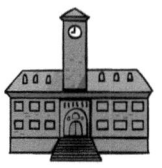

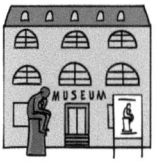

美術館

museum

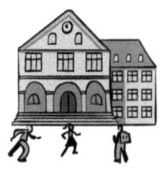

学校

school

大学

university

銀行

bank

病院

hospital

ホテル

hotel

薬局

pharmacy

オフィス

office

書店

book shop

ショップ

shop

花屋

flower shop

スーパーマーケット

supermarket

市場

market

デパート

department store

魚屋

fishmonger's shop

ショッピングセンター

mall

港

harbor

公園

park

ベンチ

bench

橋

bridge

階段

stairs

地下鉄

subway

トンネル

tunnel

バス停

bus stop

バー

bar

レストラン

restaurant

ポスト

postbox

道路標識

street sign

パーキングメーター

parking meter

動物園

zoo

スイミングプール

swimming pool

モスク

mosque

農場

farm

汚染

pollution

墓地

cemetery

教会

church

遊び場

playground

寺

temple

風景

landscape

葉
leaf

道標
signpost

道
path

草地
meadow

石
stone

ハイカー
hiker

木
tree

川
river

草
grass

花
flower

風景 - landscape

谷

valley

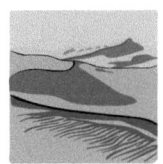

山

hill

湖

lake

森

forest

砂漠

desert

火山

volcano

城

castle

虹

rainbow

キノコ

mushroom

ヤシの木

palm tree

蚊

mosquito

ハエ

fly

蟻

ant

ミツバチ

bee

クモ

spider

カブトムシ

beetle

蛙

frog

リス

squirrel

ハリネズミ

hedgehog

ウサギ

hare

フクロウ

owl

鳥

bird

白鳥

swan

雄豚

boar

鹿

deer

ヘラジカ

moose

ダム

dam

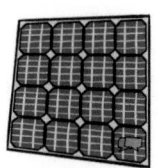

風力タービン

wind turbine

ソーラーパネル

solar panel

気候

climate

レストラン
restaurant

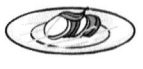

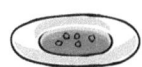

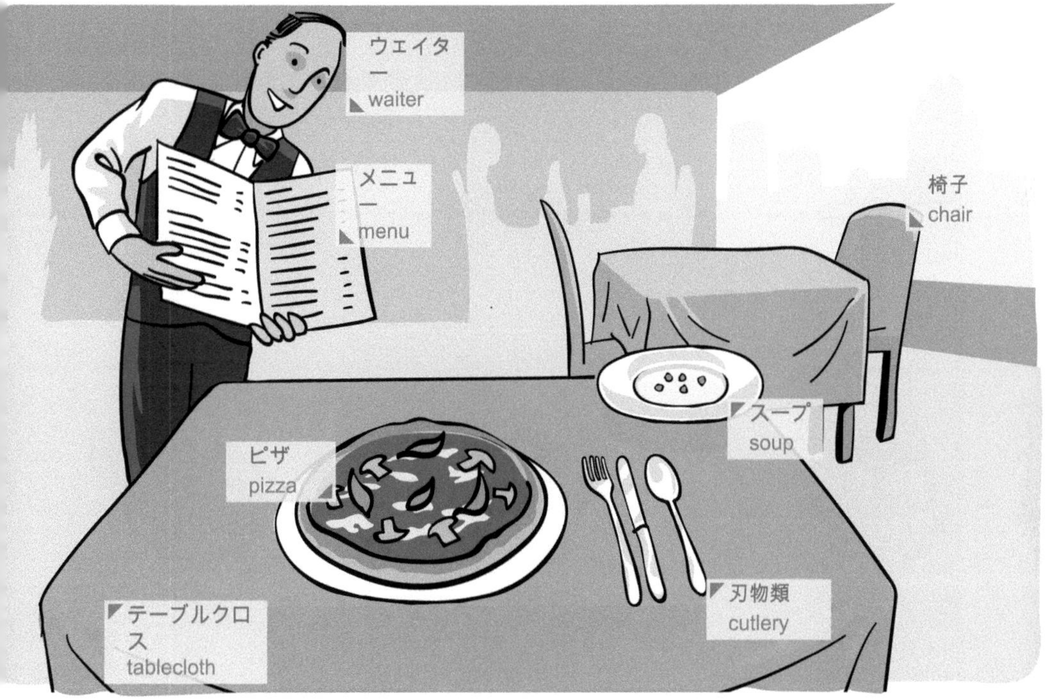

ウェイター
waiter
メニュー
menu
椅子
chair
スープ
soup
ピザ
pizza
刃物類
cutlery
テーブルクロス
tablecloth

前菜
starter

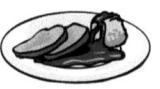

メインコース
main course

デザート
dessert

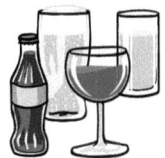

飲み物
drinks

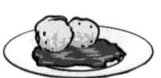

食べ物
food

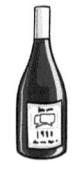

ボトル
bottle

ファストフード

fast food

屋台の食べ物

street food

ティーポット

teapot

砂糖入れ

sugar bowl

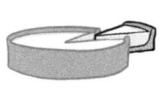

一人前

portion

エスプレッソマシン

espresso machine

幼児用食事椅子

high chair

請求書

bill

トレー

tray

ナイフ

knife

フォーク

fork

スプーン

spoon

ティースプーン

teaspoon

ナプキン

serviette

グラス

glass

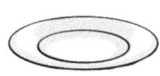

皿

plate

スープ皿

soup plate

受け皿

saucer

ソース

sauce

塩入れ

salt shaker

ペッパーミル

pepper mill

酢

vinegar

油

oil

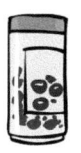

スパイス

spices

ケチャップ

ketchup

マスタード

mustard

マヨネーズ

mayonnaise

スーパーマーケット

supermarket

特価品
special offer
FOR
顧客
customer
乳製品
dairy products
果物
fruit
ショッピング・カート
shopping cart

BUTCHERS

肉屋

butcher's shop

BAKERY

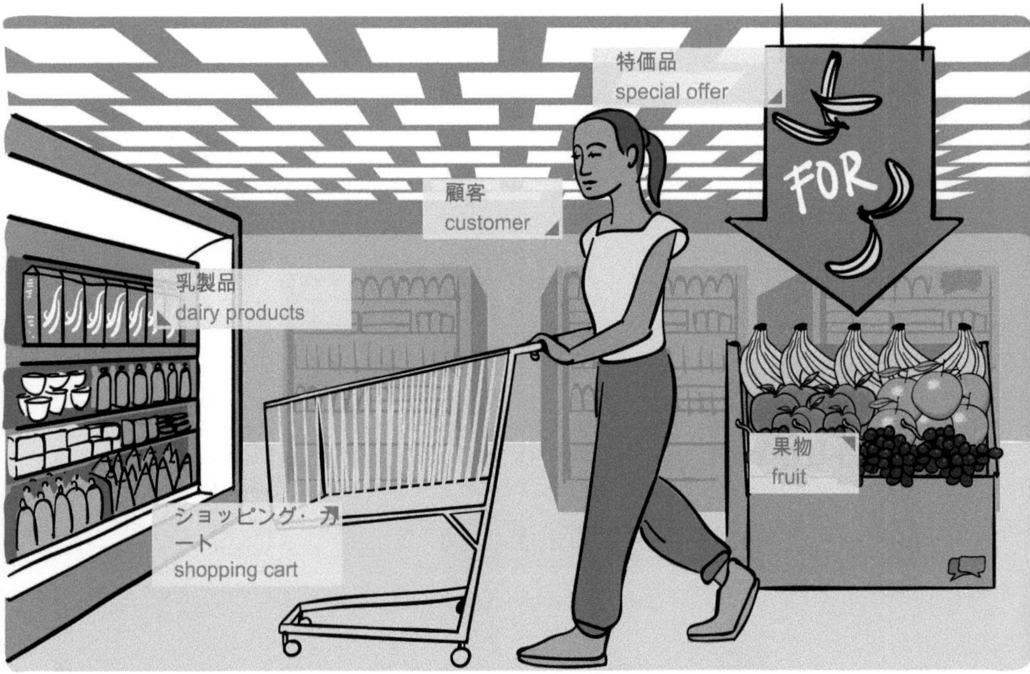

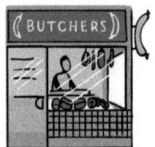

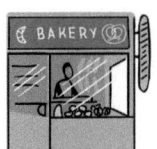

パン屋

bakery

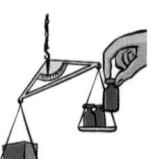

重さをはかる

weigh

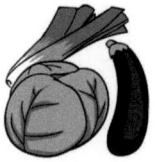

野菜

vegetables

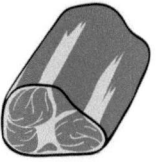

肉

meat

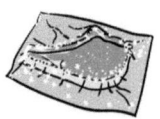

冷凍食品

frozen food

冷肉の薄切り

cold cuts

缶詰食品

canned food

菓子

candy

家庭用品

household products

清掃用品

cleaning products

販売員

sales representative

現金箱

cash register

レジ係

cashier

買い物リスト

shopping list

開館時刻

opening hours

財布

wallet

クレジットカード

credit card

バッグ

bag

ポリ袋

plastic bag

スーパーマーケット - supermarket

水

water

ジュース

juice

牛乳

milk

コーラ

coke

ワイン

wine

ビール

beer

アルコール

alcohol

ココア

cocoa

紅茶

tea

コーヒー

coffee

エスプレッソ

espresso

カプチーノ

cappuccino

バナナ

banana

リンゴ

apple

オレンジ

orange

メロン

melon

レモン

lemon

ニンジン

carrot

ニンニク

garlic

竹

bamboo

玉ねぎ

onion

キノコ

mushroom

ナッツ

nuts

ヌードル

noodles

スパゲッティ

spaghetti

米

rice

サラダ

salad

フライドポテト

fries

フライドポテト

fried potatoes

ピザ

pizza

ハンバーガー

hamburger

サンドウィッチ

sandwich

カツレツ

escalope

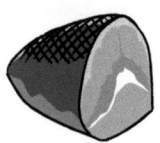

ハム

ham

サラミ

salami

ソーセージ

sausage

鶏肉

chicken

焼き

roast

魚

fish

麦のお粥

porridge oats

ムーズリ

muesli

コーンフレーク

cornflakes

小麦粉

flour

クロワッサン

croissant

ロールパン

bread roll

パン

bread

トースト

toast

ビスケット

cookies

バター

butter

カッテージチーズ

curd

ケーキ

cake

卵

egg

目玉焼き

fried egg

チーズ

cheese

アイスクリーム

ice cream

砂糖

sugar

はちみつ

honey

ジャム

jelly

ヌガークリーム

nougat cream

カレー

curry

農場
farm

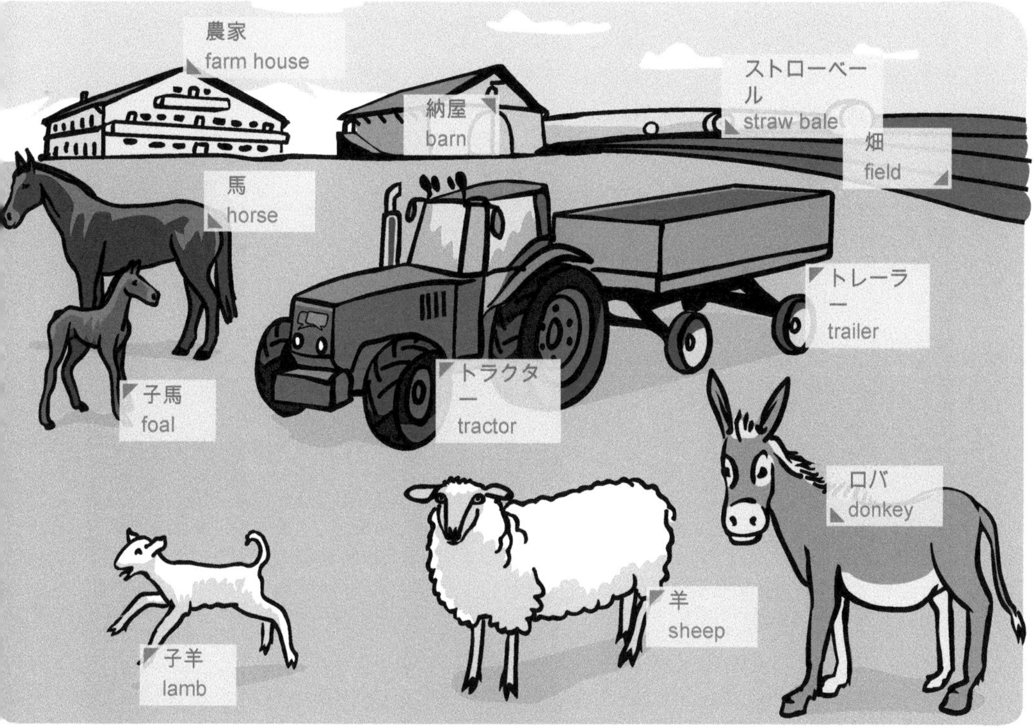
農家
farm house
納屋
barn
ストローベール
straw bale
畑
field
馬
horse
トレーラー
trailer
子馬
foal
トラクター
tractor
ロバ
donkey
羊
sheep
子羊
lamb

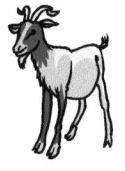

ヤギ

goat

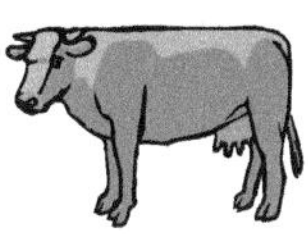

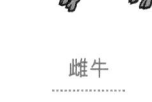

雌牛

cow

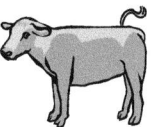

子牛

calf

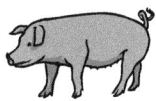

豚

pig

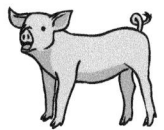

子豚

piglet

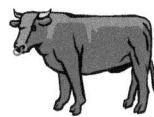

雄牛

bull

ガチョウ

goose

アヒル

duck

ひよこ

chick

にわとり

hen

おんどり

cockerel

ネズミ

rat

猫

cat

ねずみ

mouse

雄牛

ox

犬

dog

犬小屋

dog house

散水ホース

garden hose

じょうろ

watering can

大鎌

scythe

すき

plow

草刈り鎌

sickle

くわ

hoe

堆肥用フォーク

pitchfork

斧

axe

手押し車

pushcart

かいばおけ

trough

牛乳缶

milk can

袋

sack

フェンス

fence

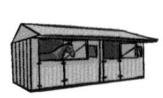

畜舎

stable

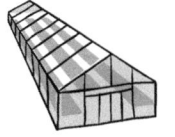

温室

greenhouse

土壌

soil

種

seed

肥料

fertilizer

コンバイン

combine harvester

農場 - farm

収穫する

harvest

収穫

harvest

ヤマイモ

yams

小麦

wheat

大豆

soya

じゃがいも

potato

トウモロコシ

corn

菜種

rapeseed

果樹

fruit tree

キャッサバ

manioc

穀物

grain

家

house

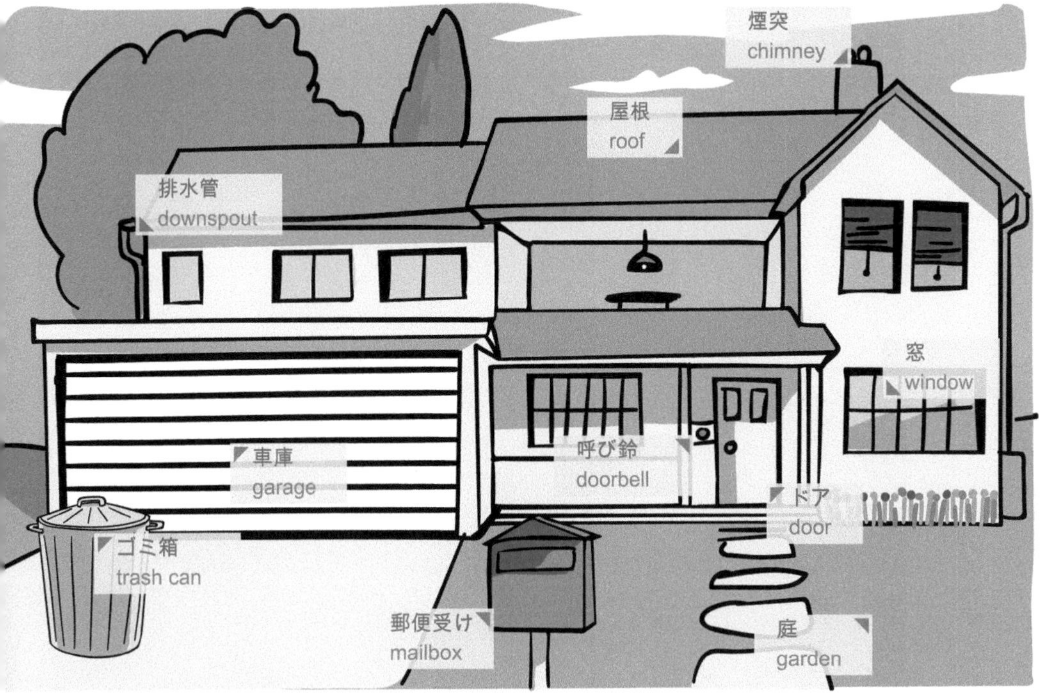

煙突
chimney
屋根
roof
排水管
downspout
窓
window
車庫
garage
呼び鈴
doorbell
ドア
door
ゴミ箱
trash can
郵便受け
mailbox
庭
garden

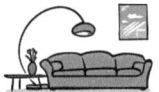

リビングルーム

living room

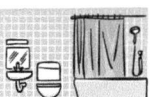

浴室

bathroom

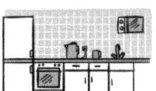

台所

kitchen

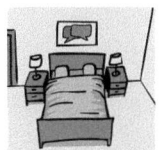

寝室

bedroom

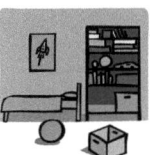

子供部屋

kids room

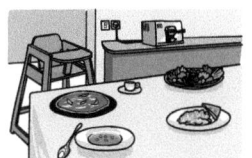

ダイニング・ルーム

dining room

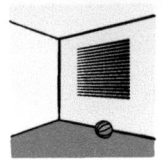

床

floor

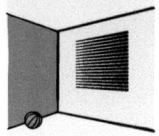

壁

wall

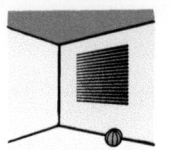

天井

ceiling

地下貯蔵庫

cellar

サウナ

sauna

バルコニー

balcony

テラス

terrace

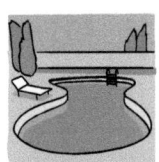

プール

pool

芝刈り機

lawn mower

シーツ

sheet

ベッドカバー

bedspread

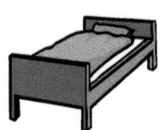

ベッド

bed

ほうき

broom

バケツ

bucket

スイッチ

switch

リビングルーム
living room

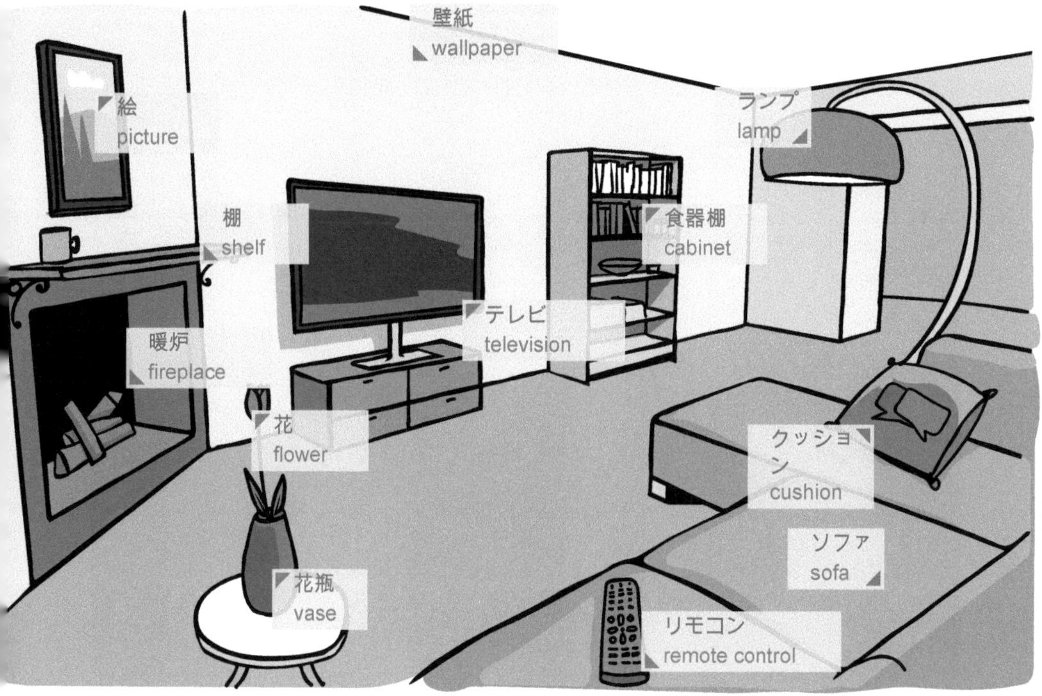
壁紙
wallpaper
絵
picture
ランプ
lamp
棚
shelf
食器棚
cabinet
テレビ
television
暖炉
fireplace
花
flower
クッション
cushion
ソファ
sofa
花瓶
vase
リモコン
remote control

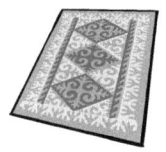

カーペット
carpet

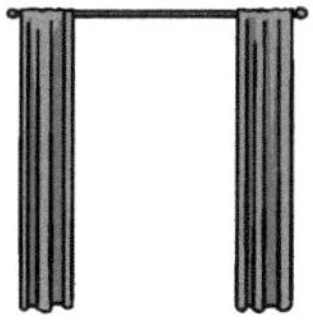

カーテン
drape

テーブル
table

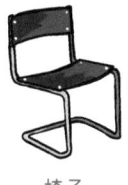

椅子
chair

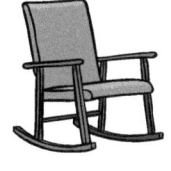

ロッキングチェア
rocking chair

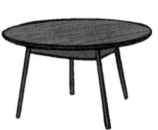

ひじ掛け椅子
armchair

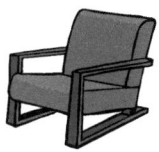

本

book

毛布

blanket

飾り

decoration

たきぎ

firewood

映画

film

ステレオ

stereo system

鍵

key

新聞

newspaper

絵画

painting

ポスター

poster

ラジオ

radio

メモ帳

notebook

掃除機

vacuum cleaner

サボテン

cactus

ろうそく

candle

台所
kitchen

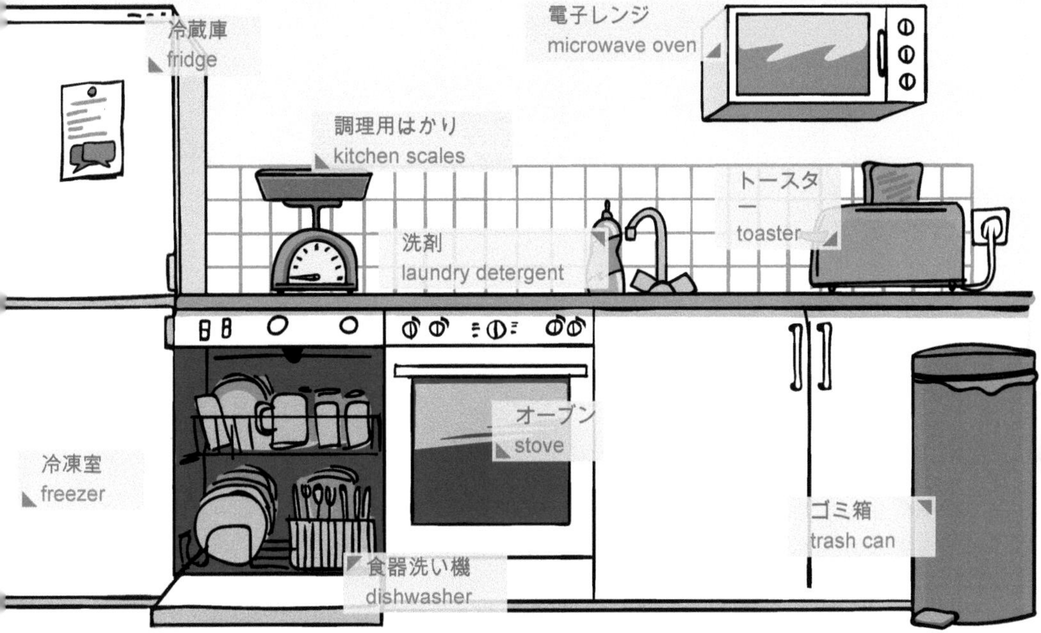

冷蔵庫
fridge
電子レンジ
microwave oven
調理用はかり
kitchen scales
トースター
toaster
洗剤
laundry detergent
オーブン
stove
冷凍室
freezer
ゴミ箱
trash can
食器洗い機
dishwasher

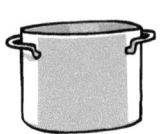

こんろ

cooker

鍋

pot

鉄鍋

cast-iron pot

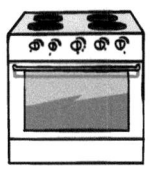

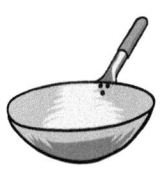

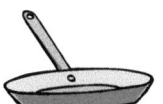

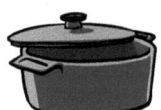

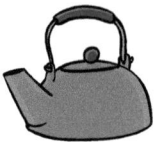

中華鍋/ カダイ鍋

wok / kadai

フライパン

pan

やかん

kettle

蒸し器

steamer

天板

baking tray

食器

crockery

マグカップ

mug

ボウル

bowl

箸

chopsticks

おたま

ladle

へら

spatula

泡立て器

whisk

こし器

strainer

ふるい

sieve

すりおろし器

grater

すり鉢

mortar

バーベキュー

barbecue

かまど

fireplace

まな板

chopping board

麺棒

rolling pin

栓抜き

corkscrew

缶

can

缶切り

can opener

鍋つかみ

oven cloth

流し

sink

ブラシ

brush

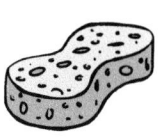

スポンジ

sponge

ミキサー

blender

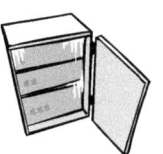

冷凍庫

deep freezer

哺乳瓶

baby bottle

蛇口

tap

浴室
bathroom

ヒーター
heating
タオル
towel
シャワー
shower
シャワーカーテン
shower curtain
泡風呂
bubble bath
浴槽
bathtub
グラス
glass
洗濯機
washing machine
蛇口
tap
タイル
tiles
おまる
potty
流し
sink

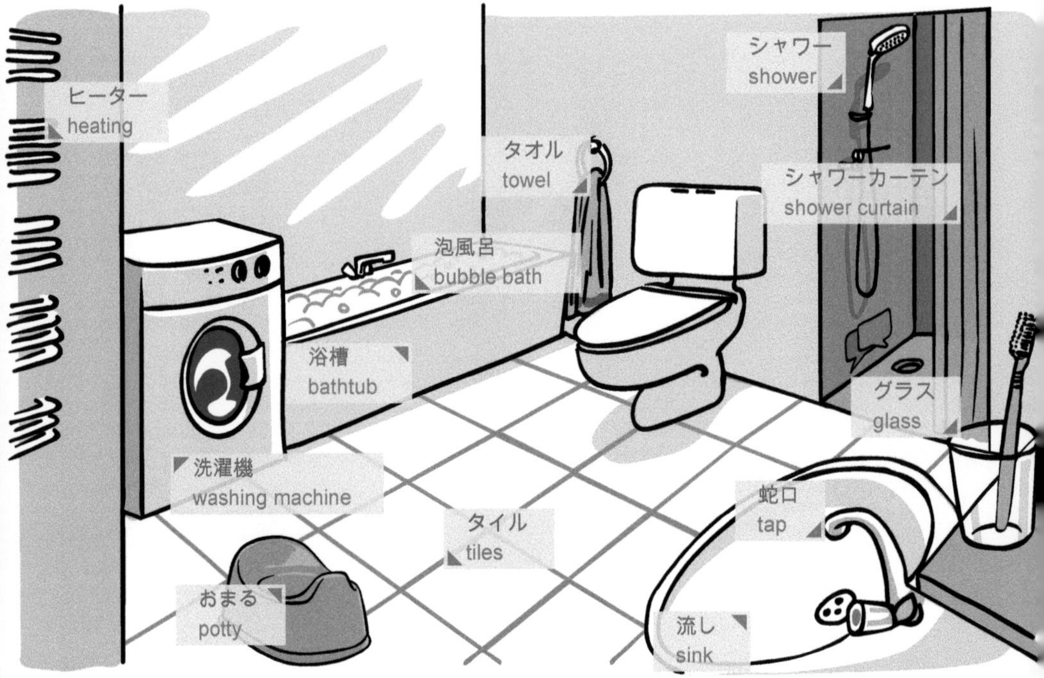

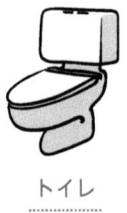

トイレ
toilet

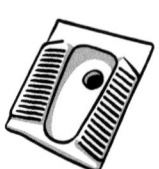

和式トイレ
squat toilet

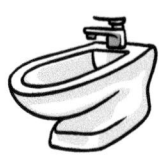

ビデ
bidet

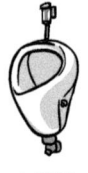

小便器
urinal

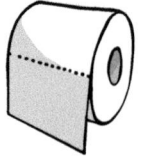

トイレットペーパー
toilet paper

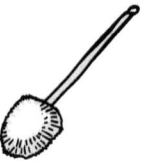

トイレブラシ
toilet brush

歯ブラシ

toothbrush

歯みがき

toothpaste

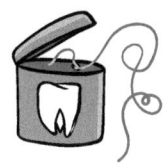

デンタルフロス

dental floss

洗う

wash

シャワーヘッド

hand shower

ハンドビデ

douche

洗面台

basin

ボディブラシ

back brush

石鹸

soap

シャワー用ジェル

shower gel

シャンプー

shampoo

浴用タオル

flannel

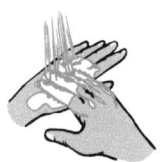

排水口

drain

クリーム

creme

消臭

deodorant

浴室 - bathroom

鏡

mirror

手鏡

hand mirror

かみそり

razor

シェービング・フォーム

shaving foam

アフターシェーブローショ
ン

aftershave

櫛

comb

ブラシ

brush

ドライヤー

hair-dryer

ヘアスプレー

hairspray

化粧

makeup

口紅

lipstick

マニキュア

nail varnish

脱脂綿

cotton wool

爪切り

nail scissors

香水

perfume

洗面用具入れ

washbag

スツール

stool

体重計

weighing scales

バスローブ

bathrobe

ゴム手袋

rubber gloves

タンポン

tampon

生理用ナプキン

sanitary towel

ケミカルトイレ

chemical toilet

子供部屋

kids room

目覚まし時計
alarm clock
ぬいぐるみ
cuddly toy
おもちゃの
自動車
toy car
がらがら
rattle
ドール・ハウス
doll's house
プレゼン
ト
present

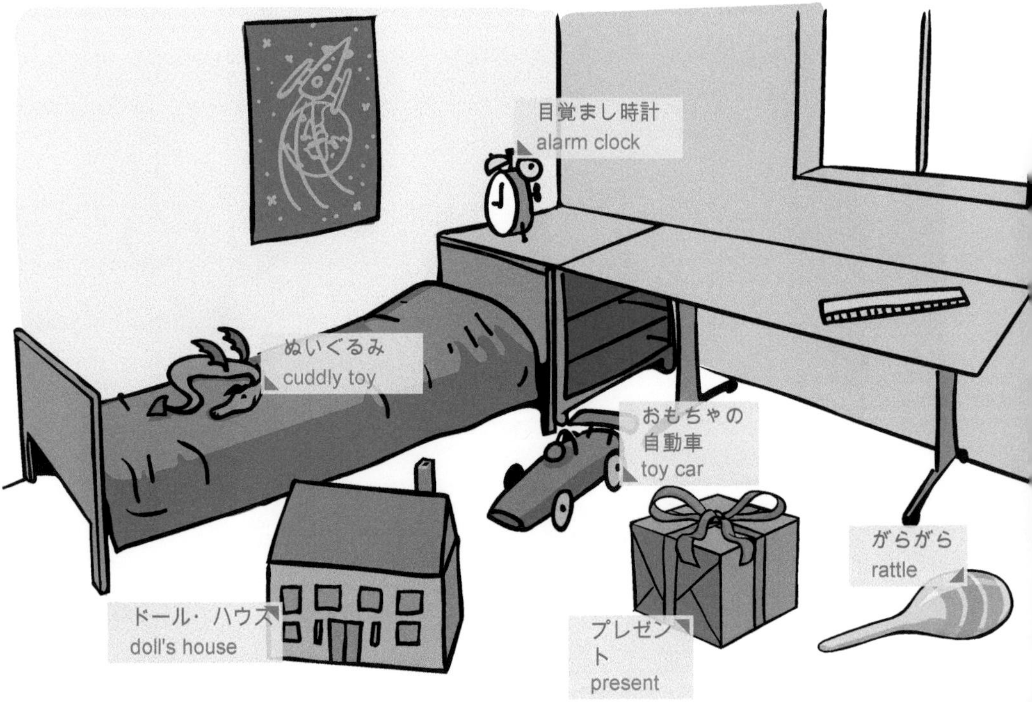

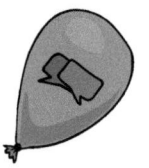

風船

balloon

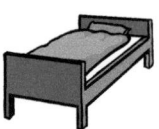

ベッド

bed

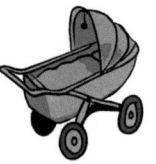

ベビーカー

stroller

カードゲーム

deck of cards

ジグソーパズル

jigsaw

SUPER
MEGA

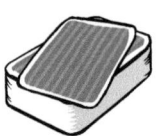

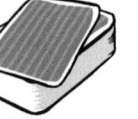

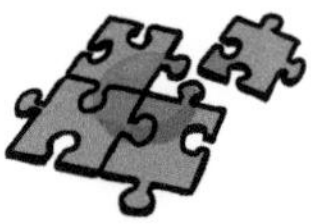

漫画

comic

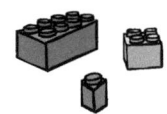

レゴ

lego bricks

玩具ブロック

toy blocks

アクションフィギュア

action figure

ロンパース

romper suit

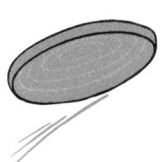

フリスビー

frisbee

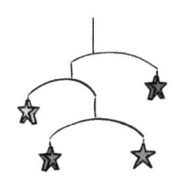

モバイル

mobile

ボードゲーム

board game

さいころ

dice

鉄道模型

model train set

おしゃぶり

pacifier

パーティー

party

絵本

picture book

ボール

ball

人形

doll

遊ぶ

play

砂場

sandpit

ブランコ

swing

おもちゃ

toys

ゲーム機

video game console

三輪車

tricycle

テディベア

teddy bear

衣装ダンス

wardrobe

衣服
clothing

靴下

socks

ストッキング

stockings

タイツ

tights

スカーフ
scarf

雨傘
umbrella

ベルト
belt

Tシャツ
t-shirt

スニーカー
sneakers

ブーツ
boots

スリッパ
slippers

サンダル
sandals

靴
shoes

ゴム長靴
rubber boots

パンツ
underwear

ブラ
bra

ベスト
undershirt

衣服 - clothing

ボディースーツ

body

ズボン

pants

ジーンズ

jeans

スカート

skirt

ブラウス

blouse

シャツ

shirt

セーター

pullover

パーカー

sweater

ブレザー

blazer

ジャケット

jacket

コート

coat

レインコート

raincoat

服装

costume

ドレス

dress

ウェディングドレス

wedding dress

スーツ
suit

ナイトガウン
nightgown

パジャマ
pajamas

サリー
sari

ヘッドスカーフ
headscarf

ターバン
turban

ブルカ
burka

カフタン
kaftan

アバヤ
abaya

水着
swimsuit

トランクス
trunks

半ズボン
shorts

スウェットスーツ
tracksuit

エプロン
apron

手袋
gloves

ボタン

button

メガネ

glasses

ブレスレット

bracelet

ネックレス

necklace

指輪

ring

イヤリング

earring

帽子

cap

ハンガー

coat hanger

帽子

hat

ネクタイ

tie

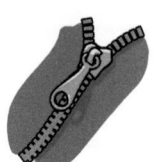

ファスナー

zip

ヘルメット

helmet

サスペンダー

braces

制服

school uniform

ユニフォーム

uniform

よだれかけ

bib

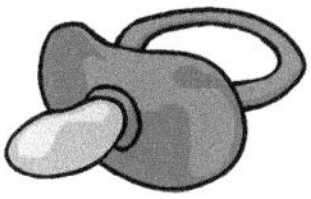

おしゃぶり

pacifier

おむつ

diaper

オフィス
office

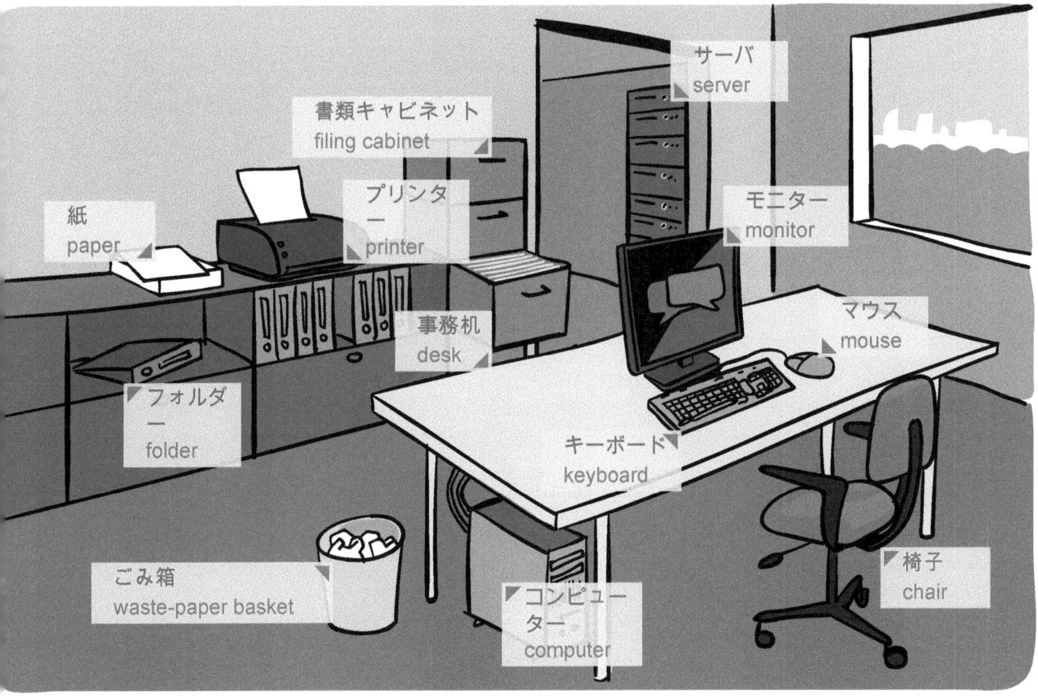

サーバ
server

書類キャビネット
filing cabinet

プリンター
printer

モニター
monitor

紙
paper

事務机
desk

マウス
mouse

フォルダー
folder

キーボード
keyboard

椅子
chair

ごみ箱
waste-paper basket

コンピューター
computer

コーヒーマグ

coffee mug

計算機

calculator

インターネット

internet

ラップトップ

laptop

手紙

letter

メッセージ

message

携帯電話

cell phone

ネットワーク

network

コピー機

photocopier

ソフトウェア

software

電話

telephone

コンセント

plug socket

ファックス

fax machine

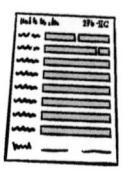

フォーム

form

書類

document

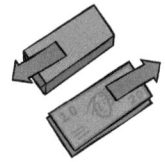

買う

buy

支払う

pay

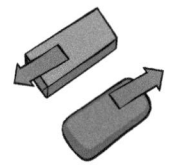

取引する

trade

お金

money

USD

ドル

dollar

EUR

ユーロ

euro

JPY

円

yen

RUB

ルーブル

rouble

CHF

スイスフラン

Swiss franc

CNY

人民元

renminbi yuan

INR

ルピー

rupee

キャッシュポイント

cash point

両替所

currency exchange office

金

gold

銀

silver

油

oil

エネルギー

energy

価格

price

契約

contract

税金

tax

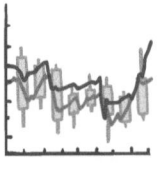

株

stock

働く

work

従業員

employee

雇用主

employer

工場

factory

ショップ

shop

職業
occupations

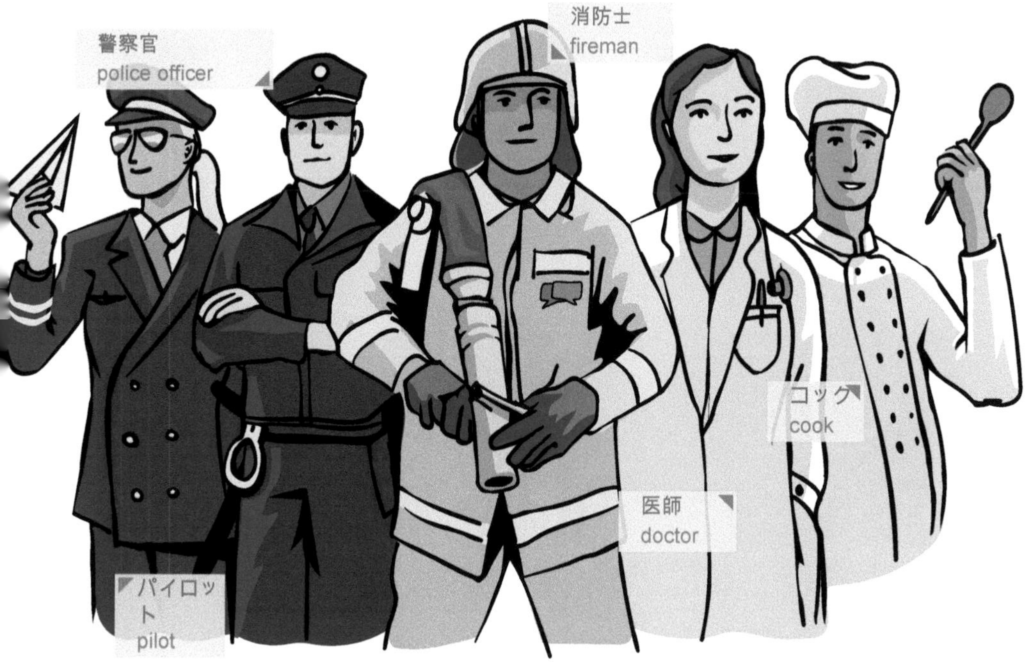
警察官
police officer
消防士
fireman
コック
cook
医師
doctor
パイロット
pilot

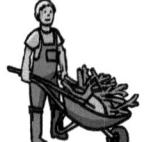

庭師

gardener

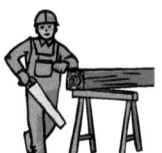

大工

carpenter

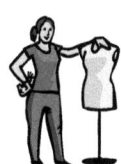

お針子

seamstress

裁判官

judge

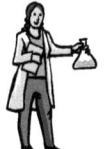

化学者

chemist

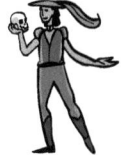

俳優

actor

バスの運転手

bus driver

タクシー運転手

taxi driver

漁師

fisherman

掃除婦

cleaning lady

屋根ふき職人

roofer

ウェイター

waiter

ハンター

hunter

塗装工

painter

パン屋

baker

電気工

electrician

建設作業員

builder

エンジニア

engineer

肉屋

butcher

配管工

plumber

郵便配達人

postman

軍人

soldier

建築家

architect

レジ係

cashier

花屋

florist

美容師

hairdresser

車掌

conductor

機械工

mechanic

キャプテン

captain

歯科医

dentist

科学者

scientist

ラビ

rabbi

イスラム導師

imam

修道士

monk

牧師

pastor

道具
tools

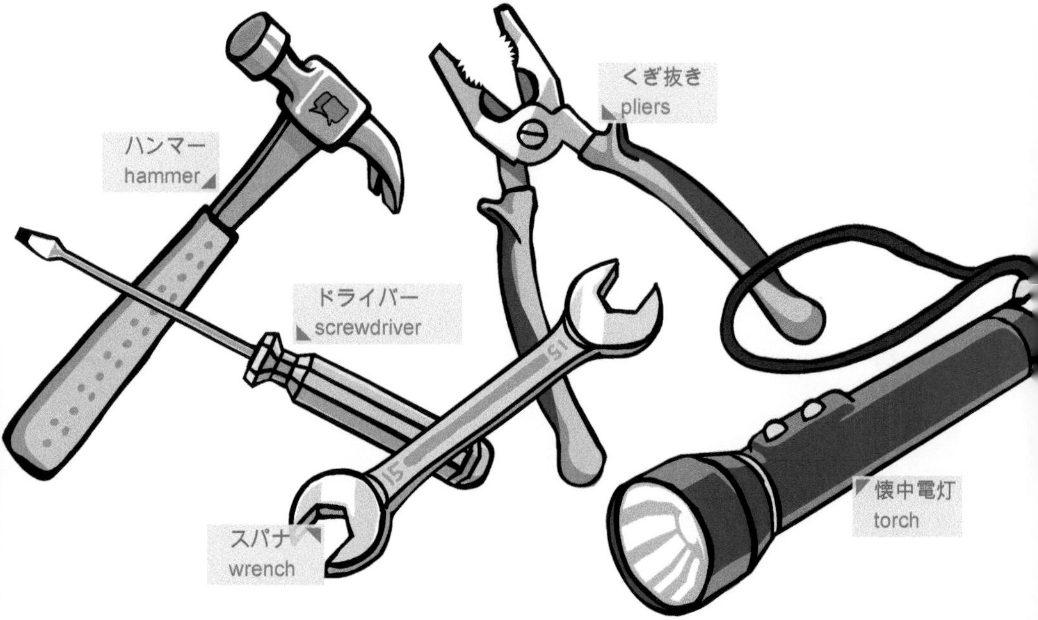
ハンマー
hammer
くぎ抜き
pliers
ドライバー
screwdriver
スパナ
wrench
懐中電灯
torch

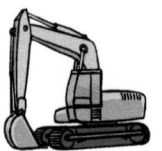

掘削機

excavator

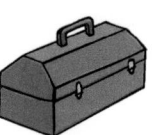

道具箱

toolbox

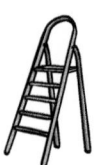

はしご

ladder

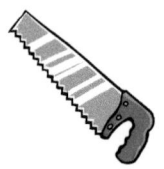

のこぎり

saw

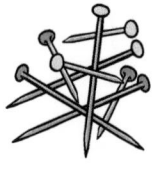

釘

nails

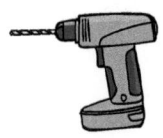

ドリル

drill

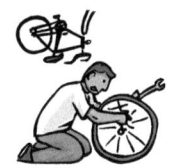

修理する

repair

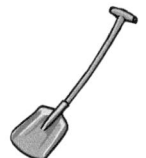

シャベル

shovel

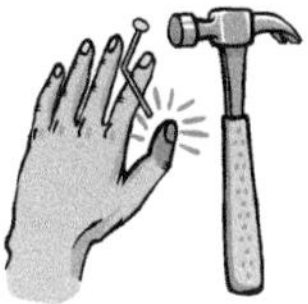

クソ！

Damn!

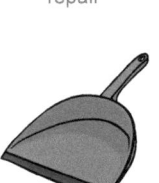

ちりとり

dustpan

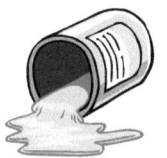

ペンキ缶

paint can

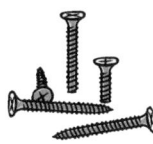

ネジ

screws

楽器
musical instruments

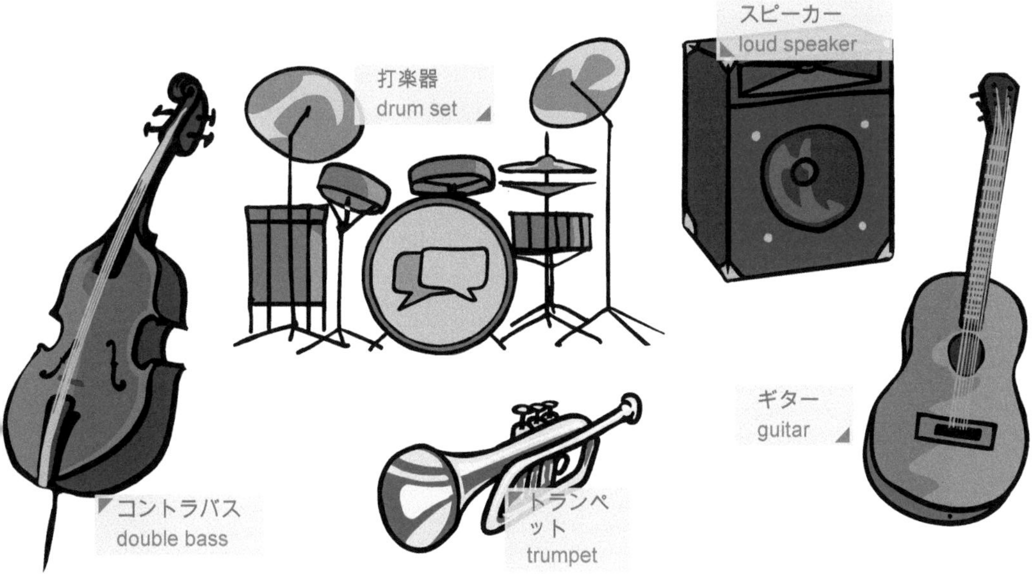
スピーカー
loud speaker
打楽器
drum set
ギター
guitar
コントラバス
double bass
トランペット
trumpet

ピアノ

piano

バイオリン

violin

バス

bass

ティンパニ

timpani

ドラム

drums

キーボード

keyboard

サックス

saxophone

フルート

flute

マイクロフォン

microphone

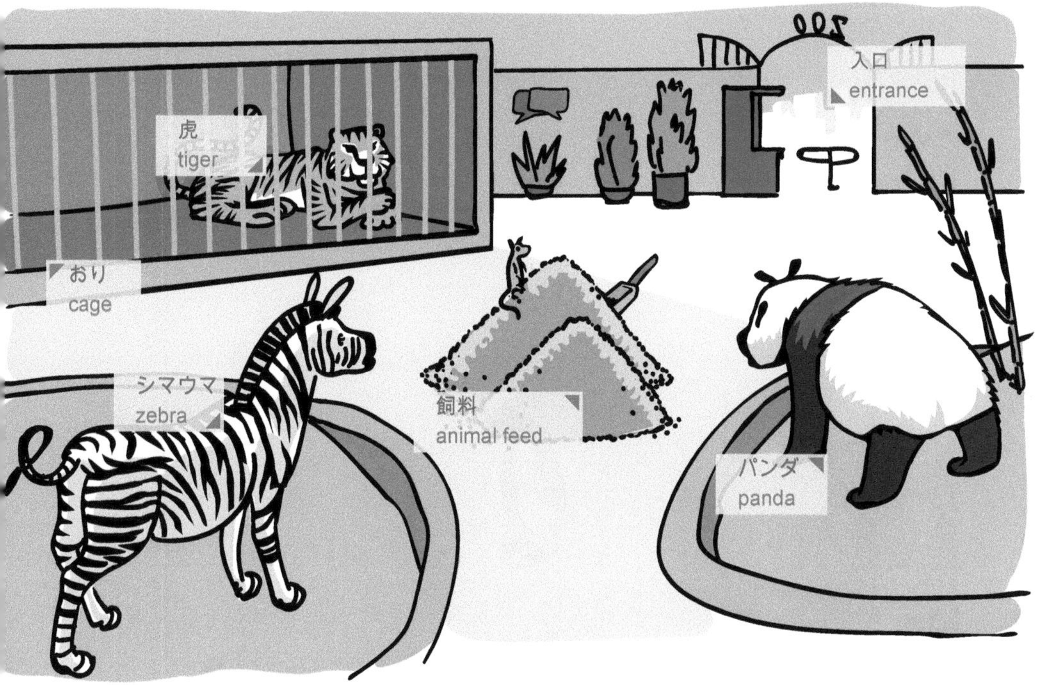

ZOO
入口
entrance
虎
tiger
おり
cage
シマウマ
zebra
飼料
animal feed
パンダ
panda

動物

animals

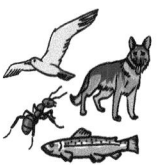

象

elephant

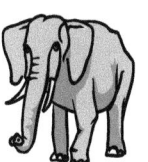

カンガルー

kangaroo

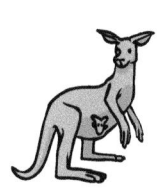

サイ

rhino

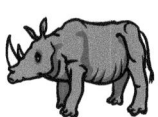

ゴリラ

gorilla

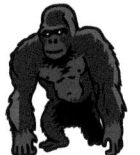

熊

bear

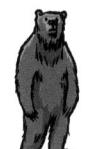

ラクダ

camel

ダチョウ

ostrich

ライオン

lion

猿

monkey

フラミンゴ

flamingo

オウム

parrot

白クマ

polar bear

ペンギン

penguin

サメ

shark

クジャク

peacock

蛇

snake

ワニ

crocodile

飼育係

zookeeper

アザラシ

seal

ジャガー

jaguar

ポニー

pony

ヒョウ

leopard

カバ

hippo

キリン

giraffe

鷲

eagle

雄豚

boar

魚

fish

亀

turtle

セイウチ

walrus

狐

fox

ガゼル

gazelle

アメフト
American football

サイクリング
cycling

テニス
tennis

バスケットボール
basketball

水泳
swimming

アイスホッケー
ice hockey

ボクシング
boxing

サッカー
soccer

バドミントン
badminton

陸上競技
athletics

ハンドボール
handball

スキー
skiing

ポロ
polo

活動

activities

笑う
laugh
跳ぶ
jump
抱きしめる
hug
歩く
walk
歌う
sing
夢見る
dream
祈る
pray
キス
kiss

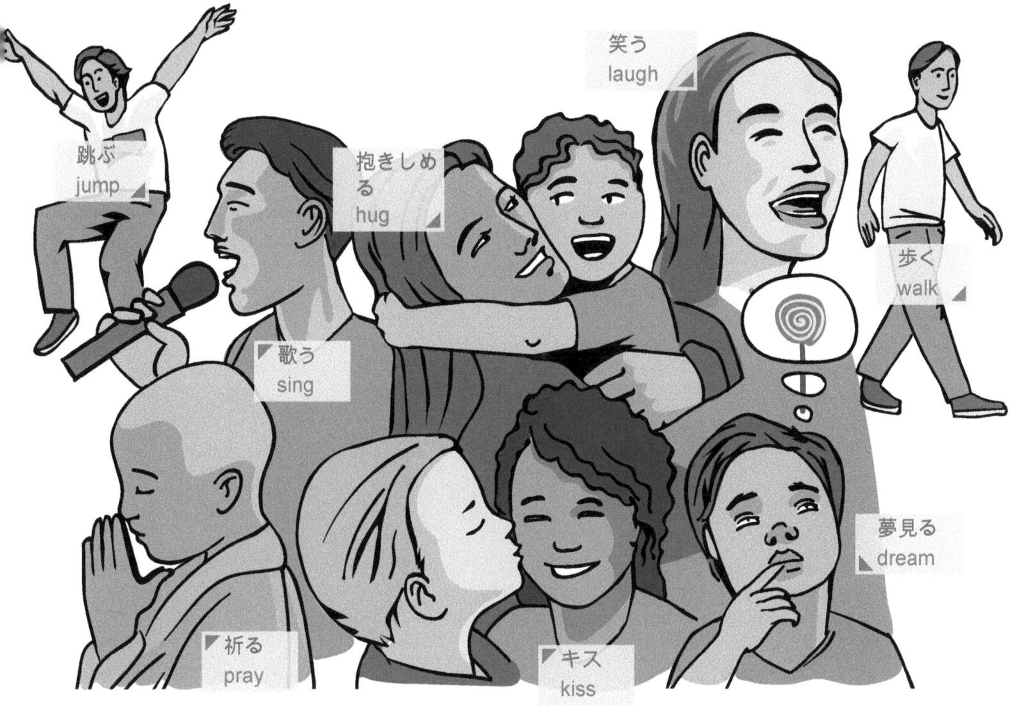

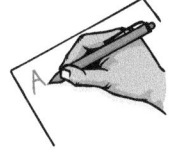

書く

write

描く

draw

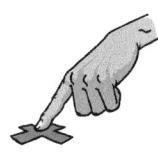

示す

show

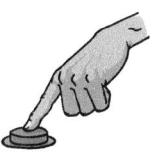

押す

push

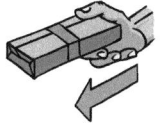

与える

give

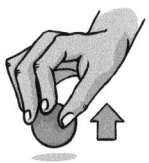

取る

take

持っている

have

する

do

ある

be

立つ

stand

走る

run

引く

pull

投げる

throw

落ちる

fall

横たわっている

lie

待つ

wait

運ぶ

carry

座る

sit

着る

get dressed

眠る

sleep

目が覚める

wake up

見る

look at

泣く

cry

なでる

stroke

櫛ですく

comb

話す

talk

理解する

understand

質問する

ask

聞く

listen

飲む

drink

食べる

eat

片づける

tidy up

愛する

love

料理する

cook

運転する

drive

飛ぶ

fly

活動 - activities

ヨットに乗る

sail

計算する

calculate

読む

read

学ぶ

learn

働く

work

結婚する

marry

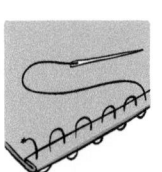

縫う

sew

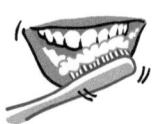

歯を磨く

brush teeth

殺す

kill

喫煙する

smoke

送る

send

祖母
grandmother

祖父
grandfather

父
father

母
mother

赤ん坊
baby

娘
daughter

息子
son

お客様
guest

おば
aunt

おじ
uncle

兄弟
brother

姉妹
sister

体

body

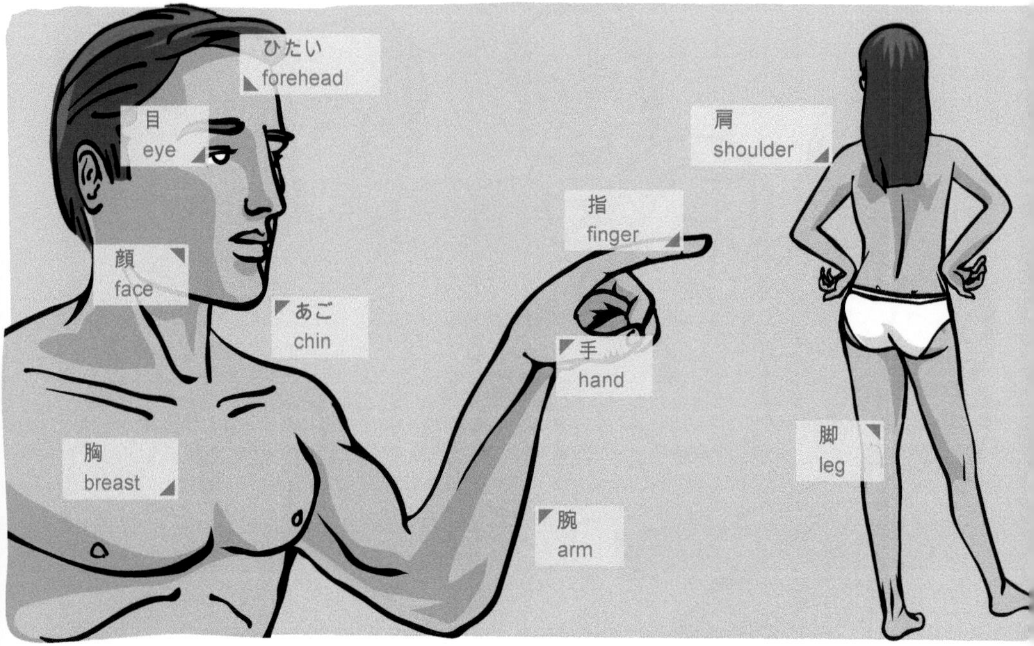

ひたい
forehead
目
eye
肩
shoulder
指
finger
顔
face
あご
chin
手
hand
脚
leg
胸
breast
腕
arm

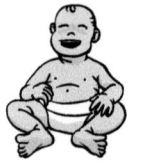

赤ん坊

baby

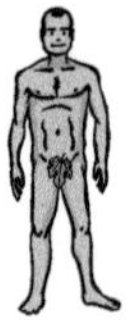

男性

man

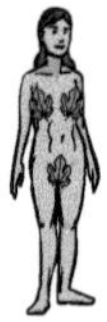

女性

woman

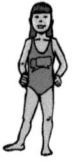

少女

girl

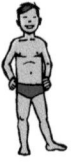

少年

boy

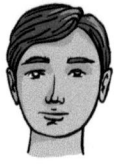

頭

head

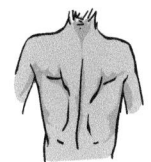

背中

back

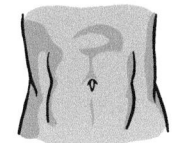

腹

belly

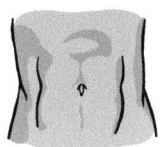

へそ

navel

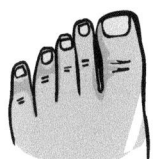

足指

toe

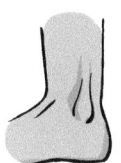

かかと

heel

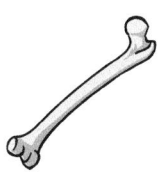

骨

bone

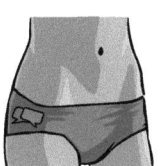

腰

hip

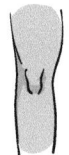

ひざ

knee

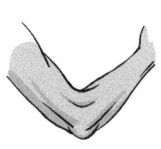

ひじ

elbow

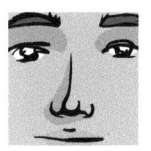

鼻

nose

尻

buttocks

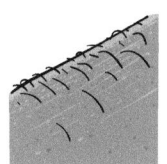

皮膚

skin

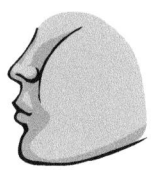

頬

cheek

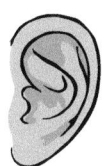

耳

ear

唇

lip

体 - body

口

mouth

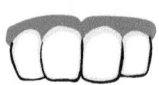

歯

tooth

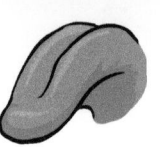

舌

tongue

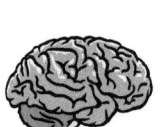

脳

brain

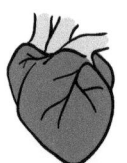

心臓

heart

筋肉

muscle

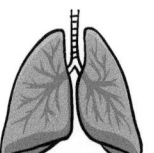

肺

lung

肝臓

liver

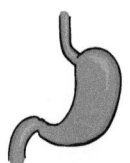

胃

stomach

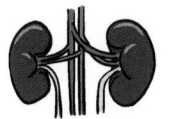

腎臓

kidneys

セックス

sex

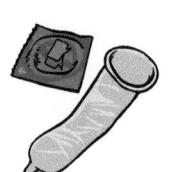

コンドーム

condom

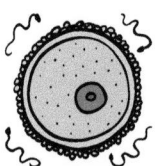

卵細胞

ovum

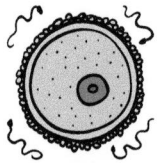

精液

semen

妊娠

pregnancy

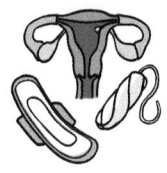

月経

menstruation

膣

vagina

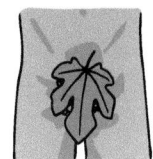

ペニス

penis

眉

eyebrow

髪

hair

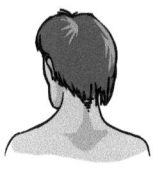

首

neck

体 - body

病院

hospital

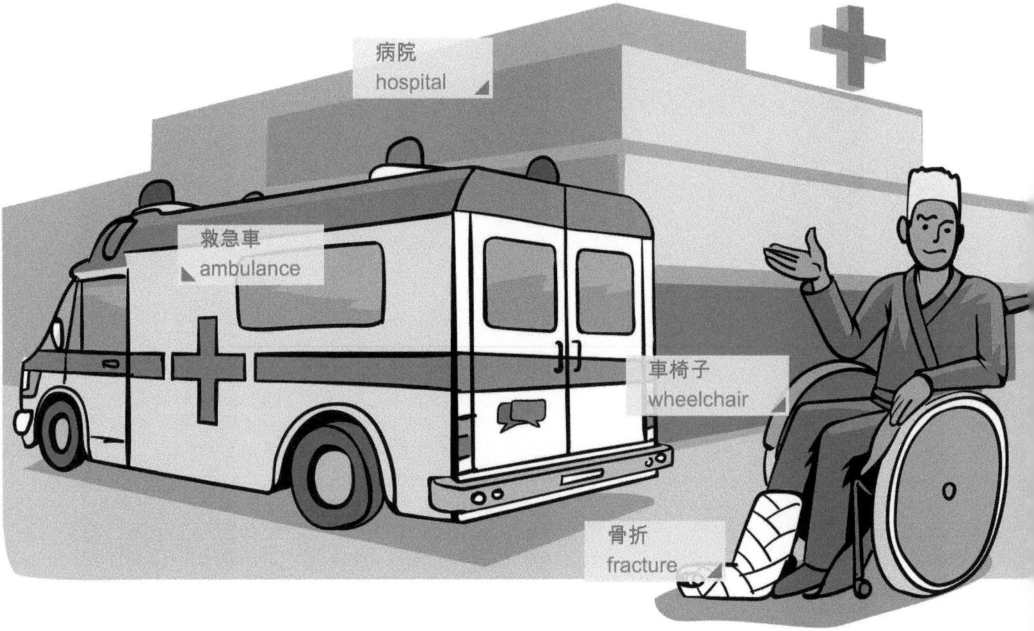

病院
hospital
救急車
ambulance
車椅子
wheelchair
骨折
fracture

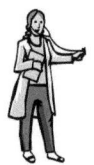

医師

doctor

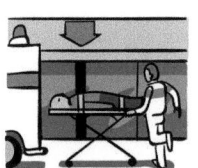

救急治療室

emergency room

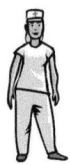

看護師

nurse

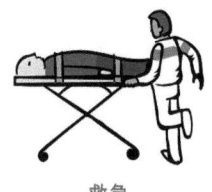

救急

emergency

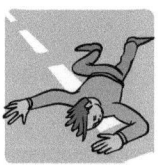

失神

unconscious

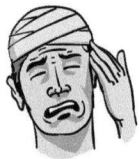

痛み

pain

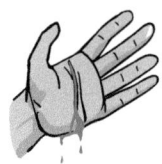

けが

injury

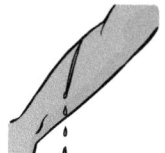

出血

bleeding

心臓発作

heart attack

脳卒中

stroke

アレルギー

allergy

咳

cough

熱

fever

インフルエンザ

flu

下痢

diarrhea

頭痛

headache

癌

cancer

糖尿病

diabetes

外科医

surgeon

外科用メス

scalpel

手術

operation

CT

CT

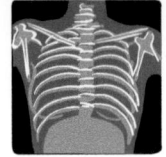

レントゲン

x-ray

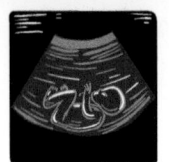

超音波

ultrasound

マスク

face mask

病気

disease

待合室

waiting room

松葉づえ

crutch

ばんそうこう

plaster

包帯

bandage

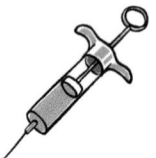

注射

injection

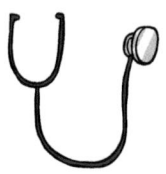

聴診器

stethoscope

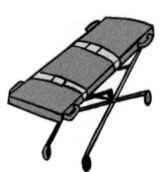

担架

stretcher

体温計

clinical thermometer

出産

birth

肥満

overweight

補聴器

hearing aid

消毒剤

disinfectant

感染

infection

ウイルス

virus

HIV / エイズ

HIV / AIDS

内服薬

medicine

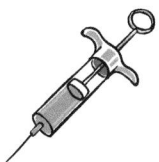

予防接種

vaccination

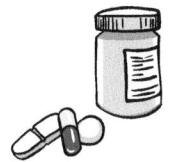

錠剤

tablets

ピル

pill

緊急電話

emergency call

血圧計

blood pressure monitor

病気の ／ 健康な

ill / healthy

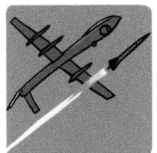

助けて！

Help!

アラーム

alarm

暴行

assault

攻撃

attack

危険

danger

非常口

emergency exit

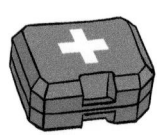

火事だ！

Fire!

消火器

fire extinguisher

事故

accident

救急箱

first-aid kit

SOS

SOS

警察

police

ヨーロッパ

Europe

北米

North America

南米

South America

アフリカ

Africa

アジア

Asia

オーストラリア

Australia

大西洋

Atlantic

太平洋

Pacific

インド洋

Indian Ocean

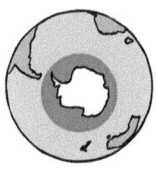

南極海

Antarctic Ocean

北極海

Arctic Ocean

北極

North pole

南極
South pole

南極大陸
Antarctica

地球
earth

陸
land

海
sea

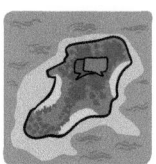

島
island

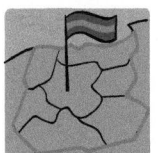

国家
nation

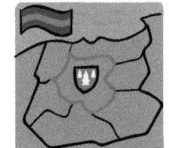

国家
state

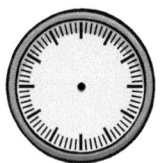

文字盤

clock face

短針

hour hand

長針

minute hand

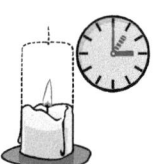

秒針

second hand

何時ですか？

What time is it?

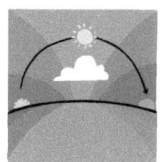

日

day

時間

time

現在

now

デジタル時計

digital watch

分

minute

時間

hour

週

week

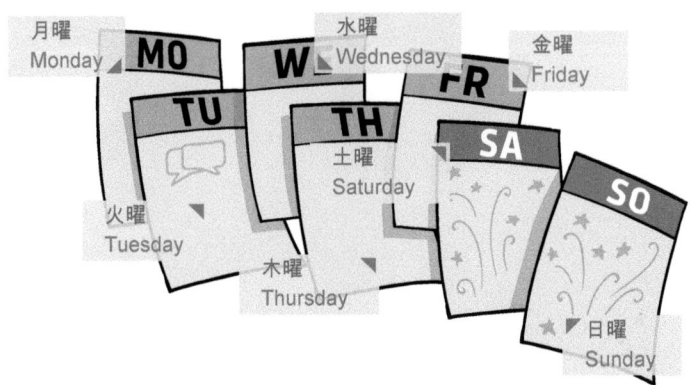

月曜 Monday
水曜 Wednesday
金曜 Friday
火曜 Tuesday
木曜 Thursday
土曜 Saturday
日曜 Sunday

昨日

yesterday

今日

today

明日

tomorrow

朝

morning

昼

noon

夜

evening

MO	TU	WE	TH	FR	SA	SU
1	2	3	4	5	6	7
8	9	10	11	12	13	14
15	16	17	18	19	20	21
22	23	24	25	26	27	28
29	30	31	1	2	3	4

営業日

workdays

MO	TU	WE	TH	FR	SA	SU
1	2	3	4	5	6	7
8	9	10	11	12	13	14
15	16	17	18	19	20	21
22	23	24	25	26	27	28
29	30	31	1	2	3	4

週末

weekend

年

year

雨
rain
虹
rainbow
風
wind
雪
snow
春
spring
秋
fall
夏
summer
冬
winter

4.APRIL 11°
5.APRIL 4°
6.APRIL 13°
7.APRIL 8°
8.APRIL 10°

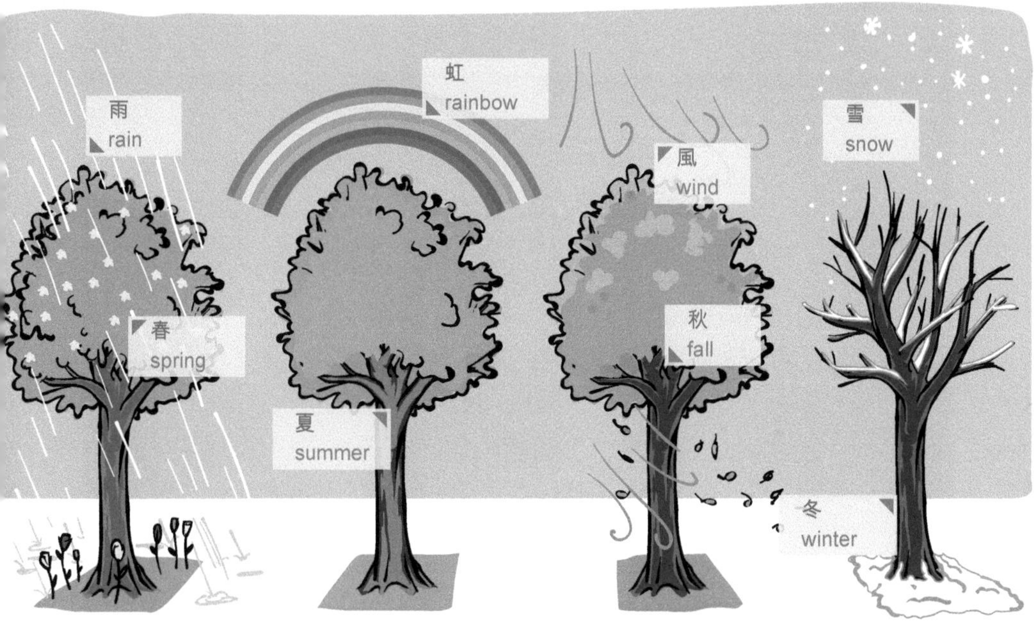

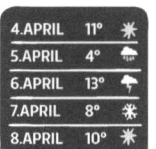

天気予報

weather forecast

F C
120 40
90 30
60 20
30 10
0 0
-30 -10
-20

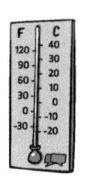

温度計

thermometer

日差し

sunshine

雲

cloud

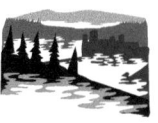

霧

fog

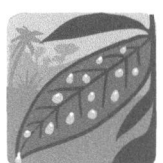

湿度

humidity

雷

lightning

雷

thunder

嵐

storm

ひょう

hail

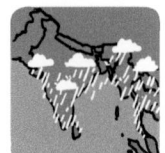

季節風

monsoon

洪水

flood

氷

ice

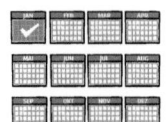

1月

January

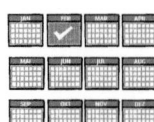

2月

February

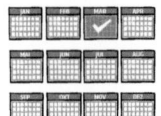

3月

March

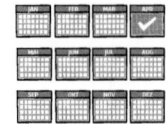

4月

April

5月

May

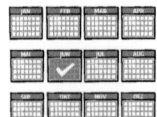

6月

June

7月

July

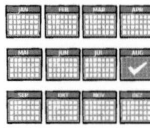

8月

August

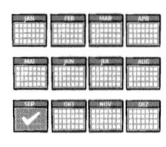

9月

September

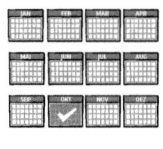

10月

October

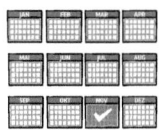

11月

November

12月

December

形
shapes

円

circle

正方形

square

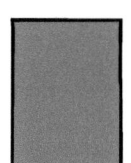

長方形

rectangle

三角

triangle

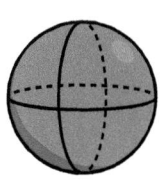

球

sphere

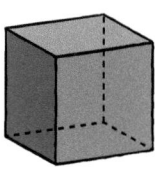

立方体

cube

白
....
white

黄
....
yellow

オレンジ
....
orange

ピンク
....
pink

赤
....
red

紫
....
purple

青
....
blue

緑
....
green

茶
....
brown

灰色
....
gray

黒
....
black

多い ／ 少ない

a lot / a little

怒っている ／
落ち着いている

angry / calm

美しい ／ 醜い

beautiful / ugly

初め ／ 終わり

beginning / end

大きい ／ 小さい

big / small

明るい ／ 暗い

bright / dark

兄弟 ／ 姉妹

brother / sister

清潔な ／ 汚い

clean / dirty

完全な ／ 不完全な

complete / incomplete

日中 ／ 夜

day / night

死んだ ／ 生きている

dead / alive

幅広い ／ 狭い

wide / narrow

食べられる /
食べられない
edible / inedible

悪意のある / 親切な
evil / kind

興奮している /
退屈している
excited / bored

太った / 痩せた
fat / thin

最初に / 最後に
first / last

友人 / 敵
friend / enemy

いっぱいの / 空の
full / empty

硬い / 柔らかい
hard / soft

重い / 軽い
heavy / light

空腹 / 喉の渇き
hunger / thirst

病気の / 健康な
ill / healthy

違法な / 合法な
illegal / legal

賢い / 愚かな
intelligent / stupid

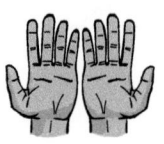

左に / 右に
left / right

近い / 遠い
near / far

新しい ／ 中古の

new / used

何もない ／ 何かある

nothing / something

老いた ／ 若い

old / young

オン ／ オフ

on / off

開いている ／
閉まっている

open / closed

静かな ／ うるさい

quiet / loud

裕福な ／ 貧乏な

rich / poor

正しい ／ 間違っている

right / wrong

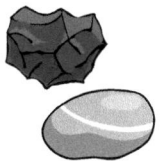

粗い ／ なめらか

rough / smooth

悲しい ／ 幸せな

sad / happy

短い ／ 長い

short / long

ゆっくり ／ 速い

slow / fast

濡れた ／ 乾いた

wet / dry

温かい ／ 冷たい

warm / cool

戦争 ／ 平和

war / peace

0

ゼロ

zero

1

1

one

2

2

two

3

3

three

4

4

four

5

5

five

6

6

six

7

7

seven

8

8

eight

9

9

nine

10

10

ten

11

11

eleven

12

12

twelve

13

13

thirteen

14

14

fourteen

15

15

fifteen

16

16

sixteen

17

17

seventeen

18

18

eighteen

19

19

nineteen

20

20

twenty

100

100

hundred

1.000

1000

thousand

1.000.000

100万

million

英語

English

アメリカ英語

American English

中国標準語

Chinese Mandarin

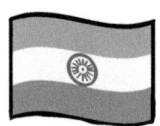

ヒンディー語

Hindi

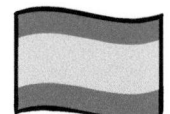

スペイン語

Spanish

フランス語

French

アラビア語

Arabic

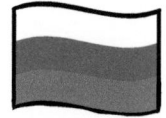

ロシア語

Russian

ポルトガル語

Portuguese

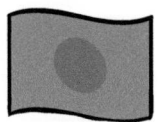

ベンガル語

Bengali

ドイツ語

German

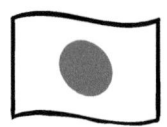

日本語

Japanese

私

I

あなた

you

彼 / 彼女 / それ

he / she / it

私たち

we

あなたたち

you

彼ら

they

誰？

who?

何？

what?

どうやって？

how?

どこ？

where?

いつ？

when?

名前

name

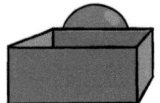

後ろ

behind

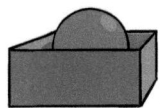

中

in

前

in front of

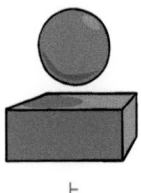

上

over

上

on

下

under

横

beside

間

between

場所

place